The Five Step Value Framework

Measuring the business value of internal communication

Corin Ashby MBA, FIIC

MOSAÏQUEPRESS

Published by
MOSAÏQUE PRESS

70 Priory Road
Kenilworth
Warwickshire
CV8 1LQ
www.mosaiquepress.com

This book is based on research carried out as part-fulfilment of
The Warwick MBA programme requirements, University of Warwick.

ISBN 978-1-906852-46-7

The Five Step Value Framework

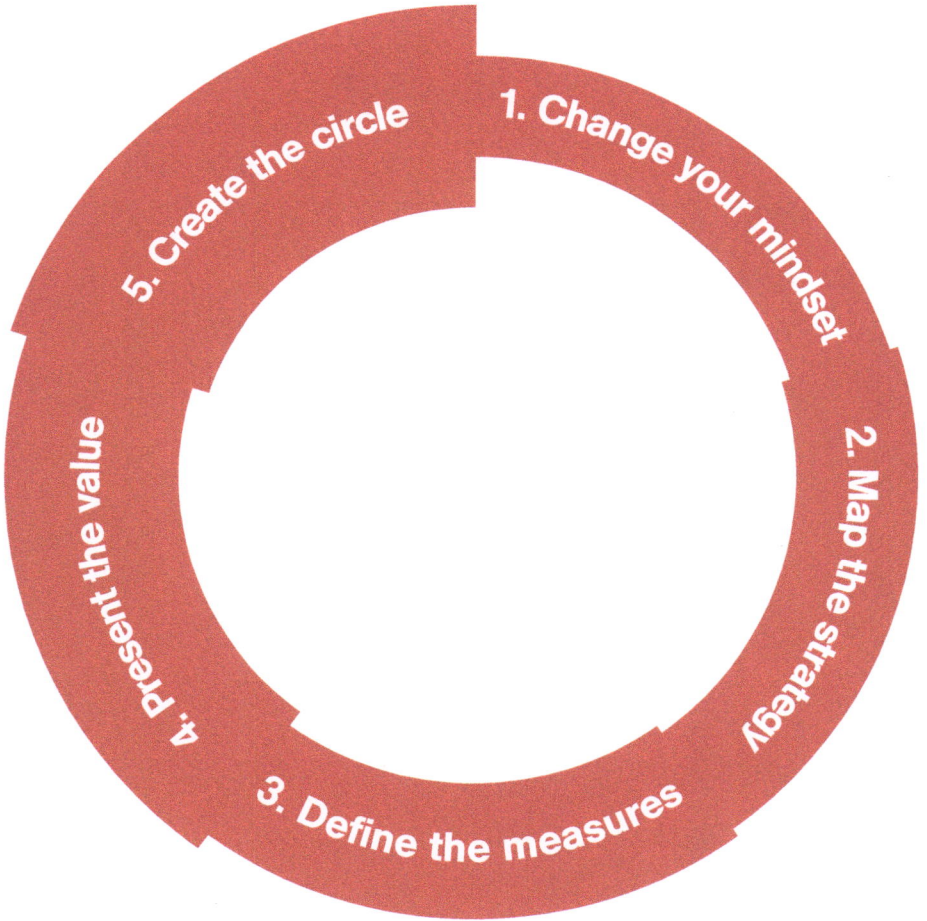

1. Change your mindset
2. Map the strategy
3. Define the measures
4. Present the value
5. Create the circle

Contents

[Internal communication must develop a robust strategic outlook in order to be taken seriously by all management levels and to demonstrate greater value to the business.]

[The best strategies are highly dynamic in nature. They are continually re-shaped to best meet the changing needs of the organisation.]

[Internal communication activity has an important part to play in extracting new ideas and innovation from the very people that understand specific processes best – the workforce.]

[Internal communicators must not be afraid to show how their function has contributed to the collective success of a particular project or a specific performance outcome.]

[All too often professional communicators overlook the best ways to communicate what they do and then wonder why greater support from management is not forthcoming.]

Executive summary

Internal Communication is commonly defined as the function responsible for effective communications among participants within an organisation. But if the value of internal communication (IC) to a business is not clear then it's not rocket science to assume organisations will be unwilling to invest significant time and resource in it.

The majority of respondents to our research cited a need for more budget and resources. But few talked about building hard, practical business cases to support such funding approvals.

Our conclusion? From the interviews we undertook we witnessed a daily devaluation of the IC function occurring within a significant majority of UK organisations. Internal communicators are running very hard just to stand still.

A way forward:

Until internal communication professionals actively measure and demonstrate the real business value of what they do to the entire management layer of their organisations, they do not stand a chance of being allotted the same amount of time, resources and importance as other functional activities.

In short, the often soft, cuddly teddy bear that can be the business function of internal communication must find a way to grow some sizeably sharp teeth. Only then will management sit up and take notice of its true potential.

Our initial research (conducted in 2005) led to a further study and the development of the Five Step Value Framework (FSVF) – a mix of measures designed to help communicators demonstrate the true value of IC activities.

The Framework draws on measurement strategies from other operational functions. Only by adopting similar ways to measure and demonstrate the value of its own operation will internal communication be able to move forward with more significance.

What is the FSVF?

In a nutshell it's a simple structure and process that enables internal communication professionals to better demonstrate the business value of what they do at a management level.

Measurement can be both a political and creative exercise. The Five Step Value Framework presented below is intended to help internal communicators structure and deliver more tangible demonstrations of business value.

The FSVF is not a definitive method. It provides a flexible framework for communicators to plan a number of measurement tactics, which combined with more traditional options, aid the overall effort of demonstrating value to the business.

Figure 1: The Five Step Value Framework

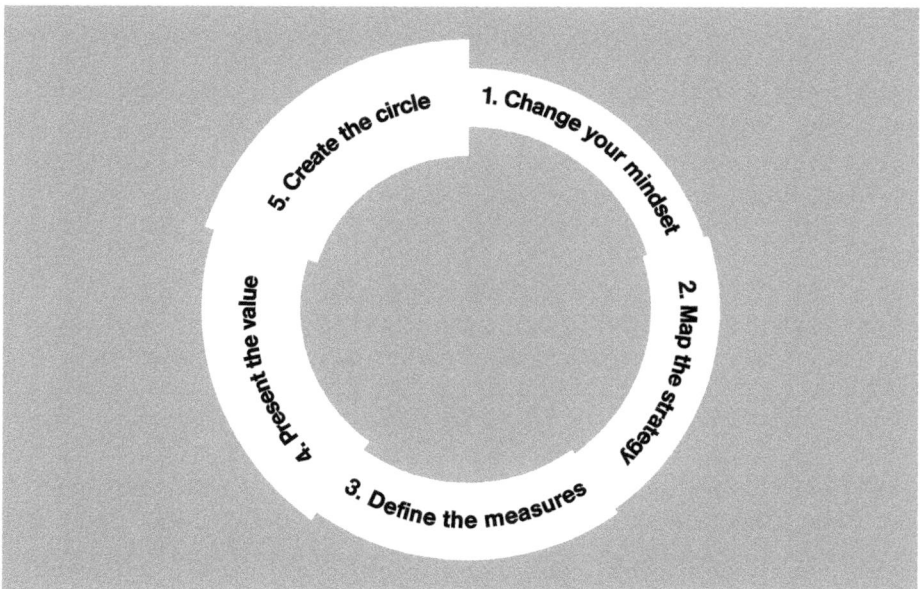

Ashby (2005)

STEP 1: Change your mindset

The first step in this process is to change the mindset of the function. The internal communication function has to be viewed like any other business operation. Operations management activity is founded on the following ethos:

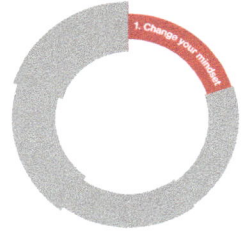

Figure 2: The Operations Ethos

Input (Resources)	Transformation (Strategy > Design > Planning & Control > Improvement)	Output (Goods & Services)

Slack & Chambers (2001)

Slack & Chambers – one of the UK's leading Operations Management specialists – hold that all business functions are operations in their own right with both 'technical' and 'operations' responsibility. Internal communication professionals are operations managers too with responsibility for producing appropriate communications strategies and managing them to agreed budgets.

Arguably, internal communication is positioned in the wrong part of the organisation to deliver significantly increased business value. Perceptions of the function are too vertically focused. There is much talk of 'top-down' and 'bottom-up' communication but critically, we all understand that the true value of internal communication comes from its facilitation of horizontal information flows.

If effective communication is truly to become the lifeblood of an organisation it should be much closer to core operations in order to contribute value. To achieve a more credible standing within their organisation, internal communicators must step away from the relative safety of senior management's wing and visibly show to their wider internal audience how their activities contribute to the collective

Figure 3: The Internal Communication Operation

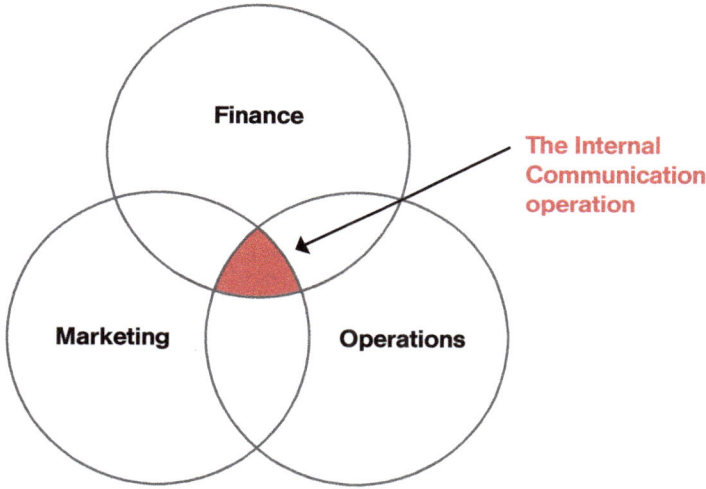

business effort. Ultimately, internal communication should be perceived within an organisation as the most basic and yet most important operation of that entity.

For internal communication to be viewed as a distinct and valuable business operation it must develop a robust strategic outlook in order to be taken seriously by all management levels and to demonstrate greater contributory business value. This entails thinking and acting like any other business operation through planning, control and continuous improvement. Therefore, it is essential for internal communicators to revisit the strategic purpose and intent of their operation.

According to Slack & Chambers there are three principal roles for any operations function:

- As an **implementer** of business strategy
- As a **support** to business strategy
- As a **driver** of business strategy

As an **implementer** of business strategy, the internal communication operation will put strategy into context for the rest of the organisation. For example, this may be the visible demonstration of a participative management culture through open and honest internal communication. It may be the communication of essential information surrounding a specific business programme or initiative.

As a **support** to the business strategy, internal communication will develop its resources with which to provide the right organisational capabilities needed to achieve desired objectives. For example, this may be the development of a company-wide intranet or team briefing system that meets the need for immediate two-way communication across departmental boundaries.

As a **driver** of business strategy, internal communication will give its organisation a longer-term competitive advantage through excellence in its operation. This is the most commonly missed objective of the function today. Any organisation that can inform, involve and inspire its employees more frequently than the competition has a significant commercial advantage. In the knowledge economy, an operation that has developed the capabilities of sharing internal and external information as quickly and as productively as possible is providing its organisation with the means to maximise success.

The classic four stage operation opposite is the strategic starting point for the internal communication operation. The description below traces the progression of the internal communication function within any organisation.

Stage 1 (Internal Neutrality) is where many poorly managed, under-resourced internal communication functions reside. They are purely reactive (at best) to the communication needs of the organisation. Their role is token only. Most effort is spent reporting filtered down senior management decisions and company events – usually well after they have happened.

Figure 4: Strategic Aspirations of the IC Operation

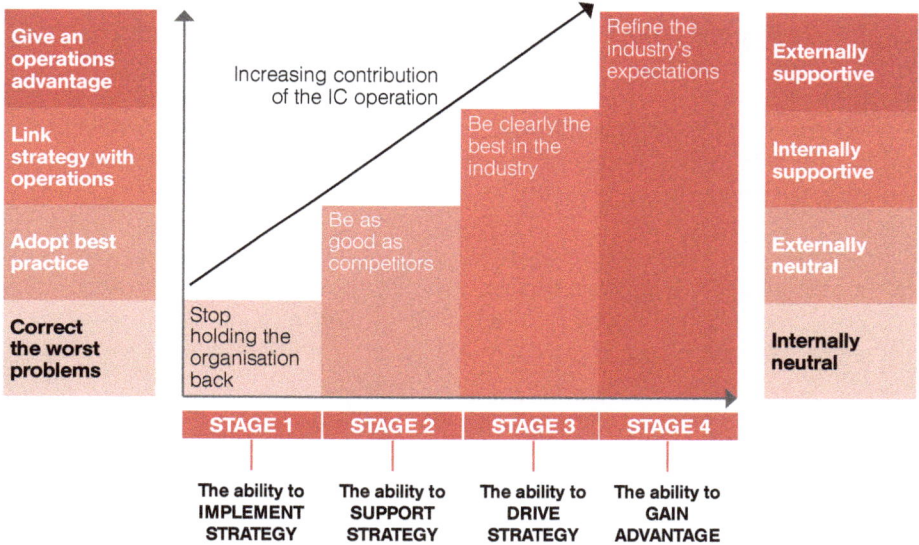

				STAGE 1	STAGE 2	STAGE 3	STAGE 4	

Give an operations advantage

Link strategy with operations

Adopt best practice

Correct the worst problems

Increasing contribution of the IC operation

Refine the industry's expectations

Be clearly the best in the industry

Be as good as competitors

Stop holding the organisation back

Externally supportive

Internally supportive

Externally neutral

Internally neutral

STAGE 1 — The ability to **IMPLEMENT STRATEGY**

STAGE 2 — The ability to **SUPPORT STRATEGY**

STAGE 3 — The ability to **DRIVE STRATEGY**

STAGE 4 — The ability to **GAIN ADVANTAGE**

Adapted from Hayes & Wheelwright (1984)

In terms of perceptions, a significant majority of employees are generally 'disaffected' by the communication output – seeing it as propaganda and largely out of date. Managers bypass the function regularly for their business critical information and see no real benefit in its overall activity. In fact, these managers see it as an internal extension of marketing or the HR function. Its costs are managed accordingly. Output is often viewed as a largely unnecessary 'nice to have' spend.

Stage 2 (External Neutrality) is where internal communication operations have begun to measure themselves across similar size and type organisations. This operation is more proactive. It adopts best practice from other organisations and has begun to establish a foundation level for all internal communication output. The need for a robust suite of communications channels has been accepted internally by the leadership.

Critically, the function enjoys a supportive relationship with senior management. There is a firmer budget in place backed by general acceptance that internal communication is a 'good thing to be doing for employees'. Employees are generally 'indifferent' toward the communication output. Feedback and involvement exists in isolated areas. 'Early adopters' within wider levels of management view internal communication to be a valuable way of gaining exposure within the organisation for their own activities but real understanding of the function's merits across the majority of management is still lacking.

Demonstration of real business value is linked to annual employee surveys. Other measurement is purely anecdotal. The success or failure of the function ultimately depends on the extent to which the senior leader or collective leadership utilise the lead internal communicator. Arguably, this is where the majority of internal communication operations reside today.

Stage 3 (Internally Supportive) is where most internal communication operations should be if they were to adopt stricter measurement criteria and proactively demonstrate their worth to the rest of the organisation. Here, the internal communication function is as good as any other in its field. A full suite of well-resourced communication channels exists that support a well-defined communications strategy which in turn supports the business strategy. All communication activity is aligned with the key business objectives as specified by both the leadership and the workforce. Activity fully addresses the perceived 'bad news' or harder business issues as well as more positive news.

Pivotal to the operation's success is the level of involvement from all quarters of the organisation. Communication channels are fed and resourced by managers and employees outside of the function itself.

Managers endorse (even champion) the concept of internal communication because they have seen the tangible benefits to the business of a more engaged workforce willing to go the extra mile to achieve the collective's objectives. Internal communication is no longer 'nice to have' – it is an important part of day-to-day operations.

At this stage, the internal communication professional operates at a more naturally strategic level. Access to all levels of the organisation is unimpaired. Their activity focuses on the development of appropriate tools and resources to support and accomplish changing business objectives. Coaching managers with their overall communication skills is continual. And over time managers' awareness of the link between employee satisfaction with customer satisfaction and overall profitability becomes a self-fulfilling prophecy. As more employees buy in to the value of internal communication, the more communications activity is generated and the more value is gained through deeper employee involvement, greater levels of productivity and higher quality.

Internal communication is now perceived as an important driver of business strategy in its own right. Strong personal relationships with leadership are still very important to the quality and speed of the internal communication operation but overall performance is assessed more objectively through a balance of hard, objective measures. This output is then shared regularly with all members of the executive team and all levels of management.

Stage 4 (Externally Supportive) is where the internal communication operation is actively redefining industry expectations. Arguably, Stage 4 is an aspiration for internal communicators but given the onset of the knowledge economy with ever more dynamic, flatter organisational structures and the growing adaptation of social media – the need to share and adapt to business-critical information is increasingly paramount.

STEP 2: Map the strategy

In order to pursue such long-term aspirations, a strategic framework is required that will enable internal communication professionals to better plan and demonstrate the value of their activities across the wider business organisation.

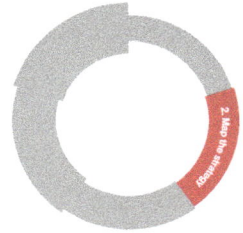

The Hill methodology (1993) is one recognised approach to forming operational strategy. The model encourages operations managers to connect to different levels of strategy within an organisation.

Figure 5: The Hill Methodology

STEP 1 →	STEP 2 →	STEP 3 →	STEP 4 →	STEP 5
Corporate objectives	**Marketing objectives**	**Identify competitive factor**	**Operations strategy – process choice**	**Operations – infrastructure**
Growth rates	Markets & segments	Price	Process technology	Functional support
Profitability	Product range	Quality	Trade-offs embodied in process	Operations planning & control systems
Return on net assets	Mix of spec	Delivery speed	Role of inventory	Work structuring
Cash flow	Volumes	Dependability	Capacity, size, timing, location	Payment systems
Financial gearing	Standardisation or customisation	Product/service range		Organisation's structure
	Rate of innovation	Product/service design		
		Brand		
		Support services		

Hill (1993)

By understanding the wider aims of the organisation and the way in which it wants to compete, operations managers can begin to put in place appropriate processes and infrastructures that best support the organisation's overall ambitions. This process is not wholly sequential. The best strategies are highly dynamic in nature. They are continually re-shaped to best meet the changing needs of the organisation.

The strategic approach for internal communication professionals is no different. They too are operational managers. Their functional activities are pointless unless channelled towards helping their organisation achieve its overall business objectives. Key characteristics of Hill's methodology are used in the following strategy mapping exercise. There are three levels to planning a strategy for internal communication:

1 Corporate level
2 Operational level
3 Value level

At the **Corporate level** time must be taken to map out the organisation's top-line Vision, Strategy and Tactics (see Figure 6). The Vision is essentially the corporate mission: a description of the ultimate destination and why the organisation wants to get there. The Strategy outlines what imperatives the organisation will focus on in order to attain the Vision. The Tactics address how the Strategy will be put into action.

Various planned programmes and initiatives with overall targets provide the Tactics for future success. Critically, communication has a key part to play in the execution of all Corporate Strategies and their accompanying Tactics. This has to be recognised at the senior level with a seat at the top table of all initiatives to enable internal communication representation and input.

Figure 6: The Corporate Level

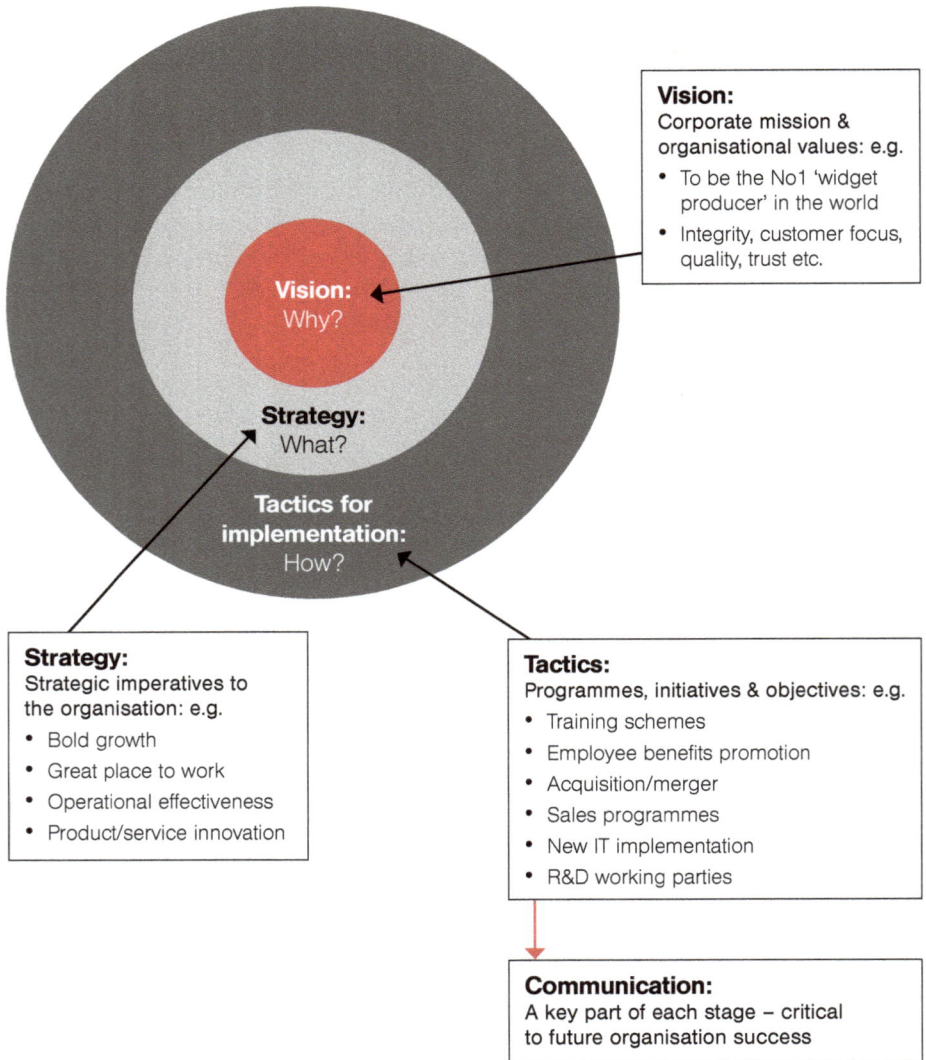

Vision:
Corporate mission &
organisational values: e.g.

- To be the No1 'widget
  producer' in the world
- Integrity, customer focus,
  quality, trust etc.

Vision:
Why?

Strategy:
What?

**Tactics for
implementation:**
How?

Strategy:
Strategic imperatives to
the organisation: e.g.

- Bold growth
- Great place to work
- Operational effectiveness
- Product/service innovation

Tactics:
Programmes, initiatives & objectives: e.g.

- Training schemes
- Employee benefits promotion
- Acquisition/merger
- Sales programmes
- New IT implementation
- R&D working parties

Communication:
A key part of each stage – critical
to future organisation success

Ashby (2005)

Figure 7: The Operational Level

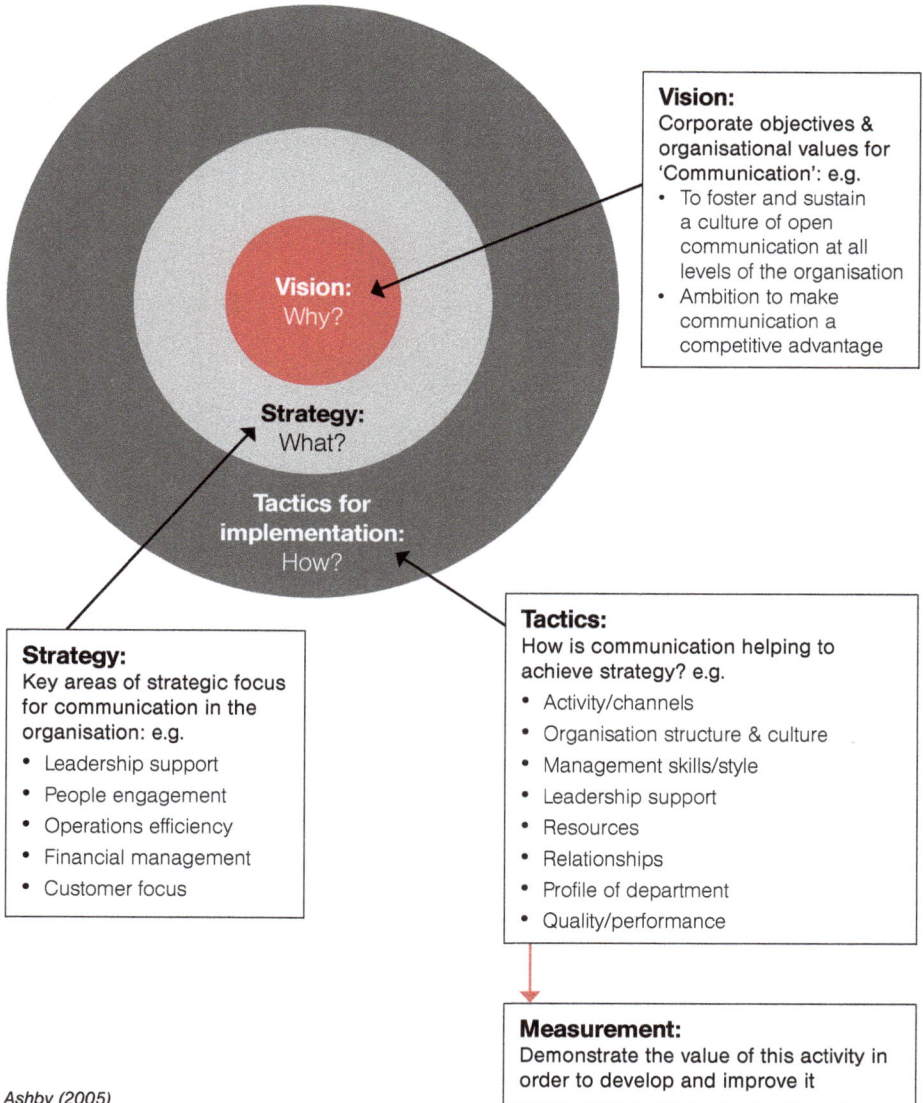

Vision:
Corporate objectives &
organisational values for
'Communication': e.g.
* To foster and sustain
  a culture of open
  communication at all
  levels of the organisation
* Ambition to make
  communication a
  competitive advantage

Vision:
Why?

Strategy:
What?

**Tactics for
implementation:**
How?

Strategy:
Key areas of strategic focus
for communication in the
organisation: e.g.
* Leadership support
* People engagement
* Operations efficiency
* Financial management
* Customer focus

Tactics:
How is communication helping to
achieve strategy? e.g.
* Activity/channels
* Organisation structure & culture
* Management skills/style
* Leadership support
* Resources
* Relationships
* Profile of department
* Quality/performance

Measurement:
Demonstrate the value of this activity in
order to develop and improve it

Ashby (2005)

Figure 8: The Value Level

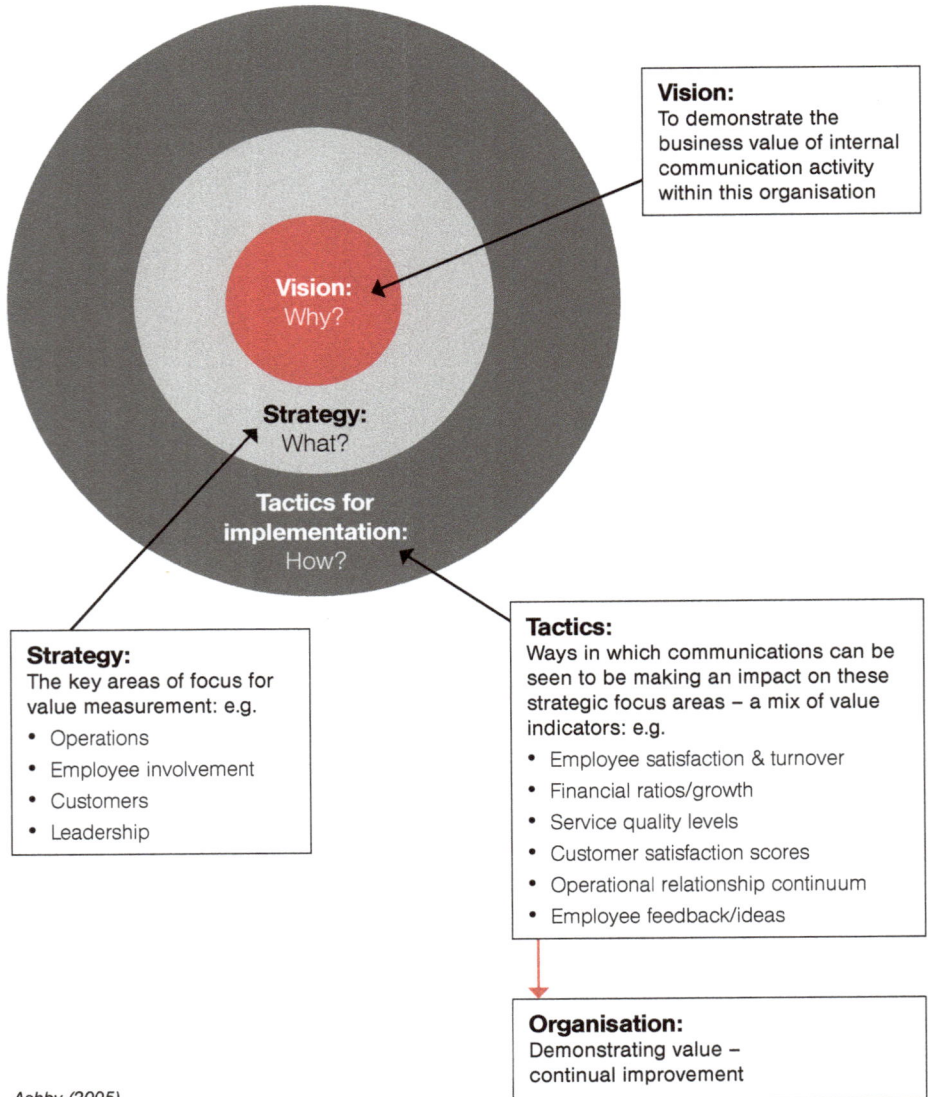

Vision:
To demonstrate the business value of internal communication activity within this organisation

Vision:
Why?

Strategy:
What?

Tactics for implementation:
How?

Strategy:
The key areas of focus for value measurement: e.g.

- Operations
- Employee involvement
- Customers
- Leadership

Tactics:
Ways in which communications can be seen to be making an impact on these strategic focus areas – a mix of value indicators: e.g.

- Employee satisfaction & turnover
- Financial ratios/growth
- Service quality levels
- Customer satisfaction scores
- Operational relationship continuum
- Employee feedback/ideas

Organisation:
Demonstrating value – continual improvement

Ashby (2005)

Once the top-line corporate picture is clear as to where the organisation intends to go then the internal communication function can look at how its activities will support and connect with the organisation at the **Operational level**. Again, this same logical structure is used to map out the operational Vision, Strategy and Tactics (see Figure 7). The Vision identifies the general corporate objectives for the operation. The Strategy outlines what the key areas of focus for the function's output are. These are aligned to the imperatives for the business as a whole.

The Tactics scope the full range of activities that the internal communication operation has at its disposal in order to influence and achieve the Strategy and ultimately, the Vision for communications in that organisation. These tactics include the development of the most appropriate communication processes, infrastructure and technology. Establishing the right channels with the right level of resources to support them is vital.

Measurement has a key part to play in demonstrating the value of each internal communication activity in order to sustain and improve the operation as a whole. This has to be recognised by the lead internal communication professional with a commitment to implement tangible measurement criteria for each internal communication activity.

At the **Value level** the same process is used to map out a strategy for measuring and demonstrating business value (see Figure 8). The Vision makes clear the need for value demonstration within the operation's activities. The formalisation of this intent through use of a strategic model is in itself the first visible sign to the rest of the organisation that the internal communication function is adopting a more practical business approach to what it does.

Results from our research highlighted some key areas of focus for internal communicators if their operations were to be successful. A subsequent process of synthesis delivered the following eight key areas of strategic focus for any internal communication function:

- Alignment with strategy
- Operational skills and performance
- Employee satisfaction and engagement
- Leadership relationships and support
- General management communication skills
- Financial support and investment
- Organisational structure and culture
- Impact on service performance

These areas are core to internal communication activities and therefore should be positioned at the heart of any internal communication measurement framework. No one 'silver bullet' measure was found to adequately gauge or demonstrate the business value of internal communication. Apparent from the project research was a need for a balance of measures. From the study, respondents confirmed that in practice they lacked a balance of measures for their activities.

Kaplan & Norton's Balanced Business Scorecard is the best-known example of a performance measurement framework, which encourages a positive mix of measures. The suggested Strategy for internal communication measurement advocates a similarly balanced approach. Opposite are the key focus areas to be measured:

Figure 9: A Balanced Approach

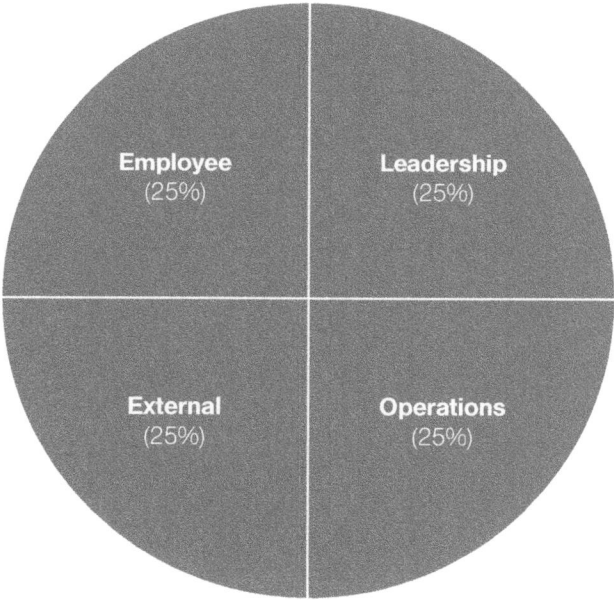

| Employee (25%) | Leadership (25%) |
| External (25%) | Operations (25%) |

Kaplan & Norton's Balanced Business Scorecard (1992)

STEP 3: Define the measures

The actual measures demonstrating business value must now be defined. The four strategically valuable quadrants ensure a balance of measures is maintained.

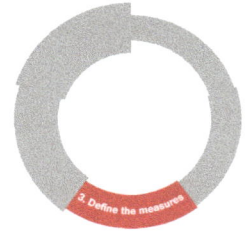

For each Value quadrant different indicators are used to collectively demonstrate business value to ensure this balance is maintained. A maximum of 25% of the total measurement and value demonstration activity is advocated per Value quadrant.

Figure 10: The Value Framework

Ashby (2005)

The value quadrants

For each quadrant, three specific focuses of value demonstration are suggested. The following summary of measures for internal communication is a generic one. It is by no means exhaustive. Other quantifiable indicators of the impact of internal communication can be used; in fact this is positively encouraged as such a framework must at all times be tailored to fit the specific needs and characteristics of the organisation it serves.

Employee: An organisation's people are at the heart of all internal communication activity. It is here where business value is clearest. Building on traditional foundations, the Employee Value quadrant of measures encompasses many of the familiar devices internal communicators employ to measure and demonstrate the value of their activities – most notably the employee satisfaction survey. But importantly, used as part of a more balanced approach, the employee survey is one measure of communications effectiveness and not the sole indicator.

It is suggested that employee attitude surveys be modified to track employee engagement levels rather than just satisfaction. This focus is more directly aligned to the business objectives. Stakeholder analysis stimulates two-way internal communication. Identifying key factors that engender employee commitment to the overall business mission and objectives (or, perhaps more importantly, issues that are preventing it) give the function enhanced strategic value. Internal communication activity has an important part to play in extracting new ideas and innovation from the very people that understand specific processes best – the workforce. Measures of employee innovation and ideas are also significant indicators of internal communication value.

Leadership: Internal communicators must improve the way they demonstrate value to the leadership level of an organisation. The research highlighted just how critical the relationship with leadership is to the internal communication function as a whole. Findings revealed how dependent internal communication activity is on adequate allocation of resources and financial investment. Significant effort must be directed at nurturing the right kind of leadership support and strengthening internal perceptions of the function across the wider management line.

Communications is a relationship business. To show value, professional communicators must put in place a systematic way of monitoring and adapting to the changing needs of executive level individuals. A degree of service flexibility must be demonstrated to senior management, as should financial acumen through accurate budget management.

Operations: As part of demonstrating business value, internal communication professionals must be able to show measurement and improvement of their own day-to-day performance. For such an intangible activity this could be perceived as very difficult. However, internal communication activity is as much an internal service as any other business process. It must utilise operational practices to scope and measure the service it provides to the rest of the organisation. The internal communication function is also a series of business processes with an input action and an output product. Therefore its actual operational performance must also be measured by key indicators and attributes. Another important, but often unseen, value activity of internal communication is the degree to which the function advises and supports various departmental project teams. This daily contribution to the collective business effort should be factored into measurement.

External: Like any other business function, internal communication cannot be too inwardly focused. This applies to how the function demonstrates business value too. Concentration on the end customer or consumer is important to internal communication as every employee is a good or bad ambassador for the company.

Business value can be shown by tracking customer satisfaction levels against employee engagement and overall profitability. To have real impact, this activity must be undertaken on a smaller scale but more regularly than once a year. Another increasingly valuable role of internal communication activity is to involve and engage alliance partners and suppliers (within an appropriate context of intellectual/commercial security). Outsourcing arrangements can often mean that organisations have large numbers of indirect employees. The internal communication function can demonstrate its value by engaging them with two-way communication as it would more traditional labour pools.

Customer: Finally, like any other business discipline, internal communication must demonstrate a dynamic outlook with a willingness to bring new ideas into its operations. This involves environmental scanning – looking at the latest advances and trends within the field of communication – then linking this back to the organisation's own internal communication challenges. If the function is exceptionally innovative in its approach then this is commercially valuable to the business. This must be reinforced to senior management and the wider workforce. Value can also be shown by comparing the organisation's own internal communication activities to that of competitors. No business operation can afford to be left behind by a more agile competitor. This applies equally to an organisation's communication operation.

The value segments: Explanation of each individual value segment follows. However, of these 12 segment examples we have chosen three extended examples where specific operations and service measurement techniques can be applied to the function of internal communication. These are suggested as new approaches in addition to traditional measures such as employee satisfaction scores and other conventional ratio analysis. These segments are:

- Leader relationships
- Stakeholder analysis
- Service quality

Figure 11: Value Segments

Examples of measures for the other value segments follow thereafter.

Leadership value quadrant

Leader relationships

Why: Careful and regular scoping of this relationship and the needs on both sides will enable proactive improvement. In classifying each leader relationship by nature and leader perspective, internal communicators can build a useful (and visible) overview of how the function is used within their organisation.

Where to look: Results of quarterly relationship mapping exercises as part of updates to senior management and line managers.

How to show: Application of Staughton's Relationship Continuum theory (2004) involves semantic differentiation scales (first pioneered by Osgood in the 1950s) to ascertain the type of relationship held with senior leader(s). These reveal:

- Comparative results of semantic differential scales showing change and improvement
- Demonstration of tangible situations in which the right behaviour has resulted in valuable improvements to communications quality and operations

Moving relations from transactional to collaborative

Like any good partnership this crucial relationship has to be worked at. Internal communicators must strive to move the nature of their leader relations from purely 'transactional' to 'collaborative' (as Figure 12 illustrates).

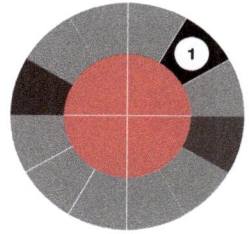

Figure 12: Leader relationships

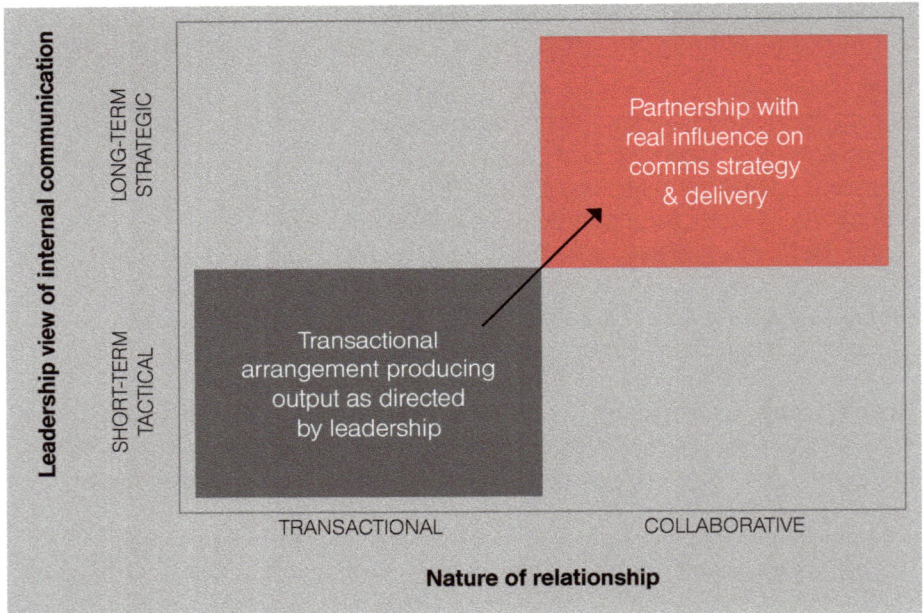

Adapted from Staughton (2004)

The internal communicator's long-term aim should be to move the type of relationship she or he holds with senior leaders from the bottom left quadrant (short-term, transactional encounters) as far as possible towards the top right window (high value, longer-term partnerships).

A simple one-to-one questionnaire like the example opposite will help to map a key relationship with a senior leader in the organisation. By regularly undertaking such an exercise, internal communicators can track and improve the quality of the service they provide to these key individuals as well as the other way around. It also enables them to position their role at a more strategic level and affords them an ideal forum with which to influence their leader's communication strategies, skills and actions.

Figure 13: Mapping relationships

METRIC	NEGATIVE EXTREME	POSITIVE EXTREME
Nature of contact	**Ad-hoc –** We talk now and again briefly	**Daily –** We talk on a daily basis sharing ideas and info
	1 2 3 4 5 6 7 8 9 10	
Importance of relationship	**Low –** It's one of many updates I have	**High –** It's absolutely critical to my role
	1 2 3 4 5 6 7 8 9 10	
Interpersonal relationships	**Stranger –** I really don't know you at all	**Partner –** You are a valued colleague and advisor
	1 2 3 4 5 6 7 8 9 10	
Way of working	**Ad-hoc –** Working with you is a real chore	**Close –** Working with you is enjoyable and fun
	1 2 3 4 5 6 7 8 9 10	
Business Value	**Dissatisfied –** I can't see how the organisation benefits from this activity at all	**Delighted –** We are creating a real business advantage here
	1 2 3 4 5 6 7 8 9 10	
Critical incidents in past quarter	**Unhappy event/situation**	**Pleasing event/situation**
	Briefly identify and discuss events or situations that have arisen in the last quarter	
Overall relationship rating	**Transactional**	**Collaborative**
	1 2 3 4 5 6 7 8 9 10	

What value?

Visible benefits: Demonstration of effort to provide leadership with as valuable a service as possible and display a willingness from the communications function to be utterly flexible and self-improving.

Hidden benefits: Increased efficiency and quality of day-to-day operations through closer working partnerships with key decision makers will ensure strategic alignment and political support.

Employee value quadrant

Stakeholder analysis

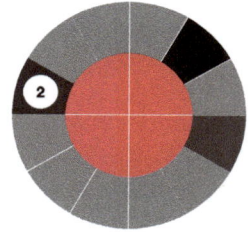

Why: To achieve real change, organisations must gauge commitment levels and also identify the motivators that work as key agents of change. Changing organisational behaviour starts and ends with consistent two-way communication. Stakeholder analyses are a variety of forums that encourage active listening by leadership.

Where to look:

- Graffiti boards
- Comment boxes
- One-to-one interviews
- Exit interviews
- Focus group sessions
- Team briefings
- Breakfast briefing sessions

How to show:

- Flow of questions and visible answers/actions from leadership
- Links to employee turnover and organisational performance
- Individual quotes and case examples
- Application of Fauvet's theory of social-dynamics (see Figures 14-18) with regard to general employee satisfaction and engagement

Social dynamics: An IC perspective

Fauvet's theory of social-dynamics can be used to anticipate an individual's role in change (Walley, 2004). Synergy is the positive energy that an individual has for the business's main objectives and initiatives. Antagonism is the negative energy the same person has for the same ambitions. Crucially, individuals can be both synergetic and antagonistic about the organisation's plans at the same time.

Figure 14: Social Dynamics

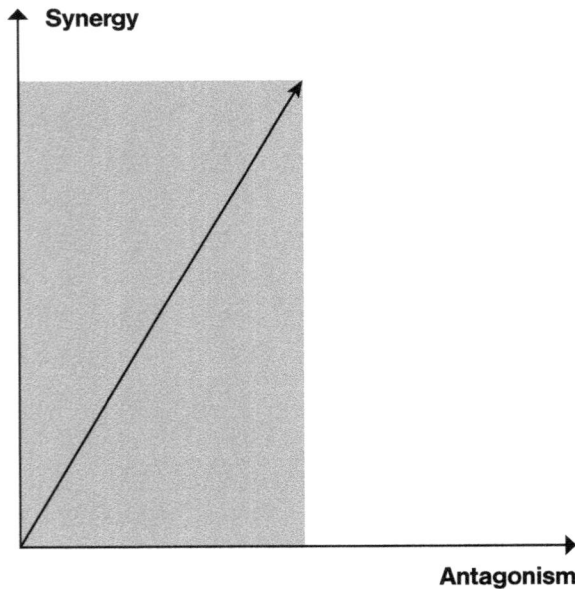

Fauvet states that this positive and negative conflict can be measured. For example, synergy can be measured in the following way:

Figure 15: Social Dynamics

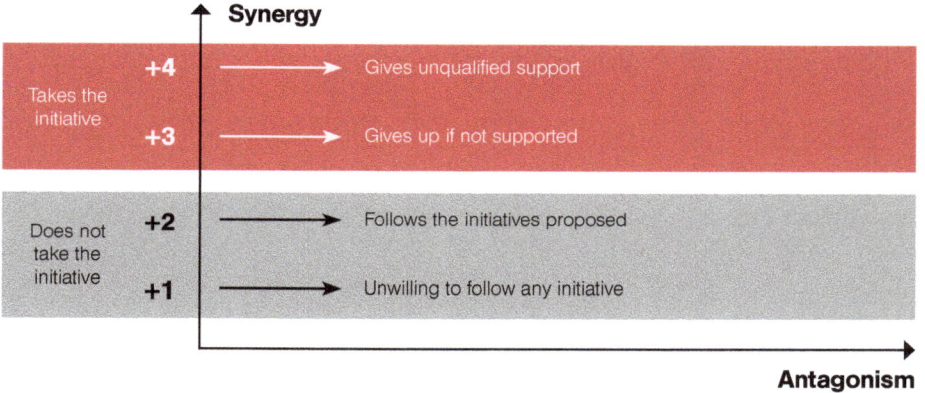

Equally, antagonism can be identified. For example:

Figure 16: Social Dynamics

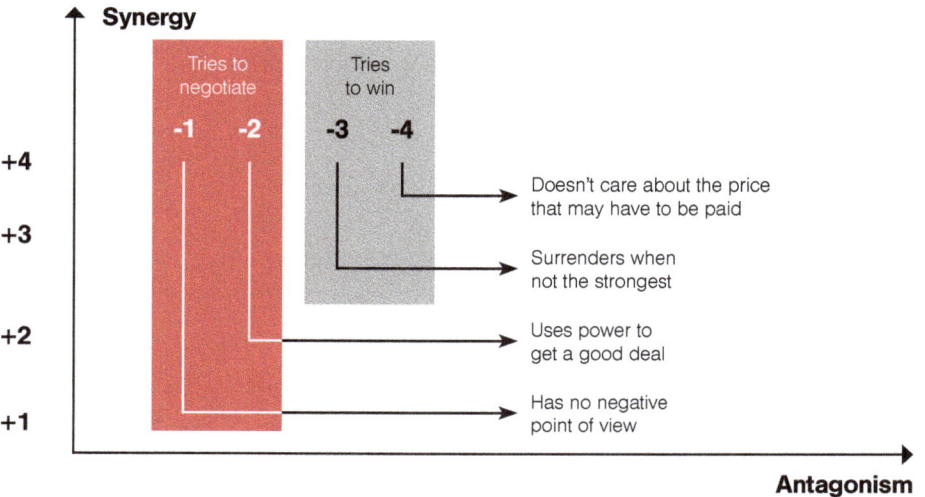

The two measures then lend themselves to a simple mapping
exercise to display the mixture of positive and negative scores.

Figure 17: Stakeholder grid

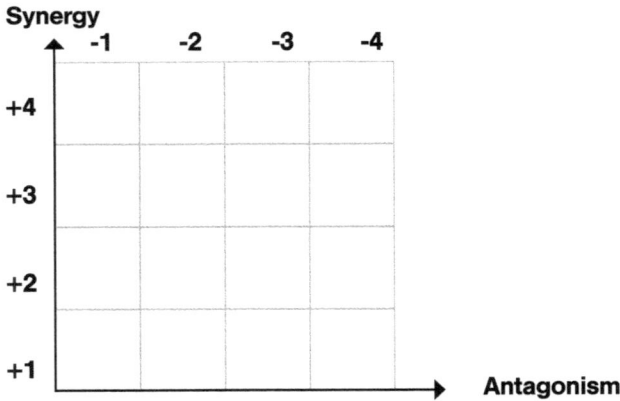

Synergy

	-1	-2	-3	-4
+4				
+3				
+2				
+1				

Antagonism

Adaptation of Fauvet's theory enables communicators to identify different types of individual who have to be managed in different ways. By mapping the various stakeholder analysis scores, internal communicators can build a picture of the make-up of their internal stakeholder audience and track how individual outlooks can be managed in order to increase positive synergistic viewpoints and ultimately, outward behaviour. A mapping exercise of this kind can be done using employee survey data or applied to a specific layer of management as part of an online conference questionnaire.

Stakeholder types:

Ze = Zealots *(These individuals are always in agreement with leadership; they won't compromise and they often fail to understand a lack of commitment from others. Opponents would call these individuals 'yes men'.)*

Communicating with Zealots: Keep them regularly informed. Their motivation must not be lost as it is crucial to success. However, their actions can indirectly destroy developed alliances with other key stakeholder groupings that are not so positive about organisational plans and changes. Internal communication efforts can be devalued (even destroyed) if Zealots are leading them because they are not credible.

Figure 18: Stakeholder types

Synergy

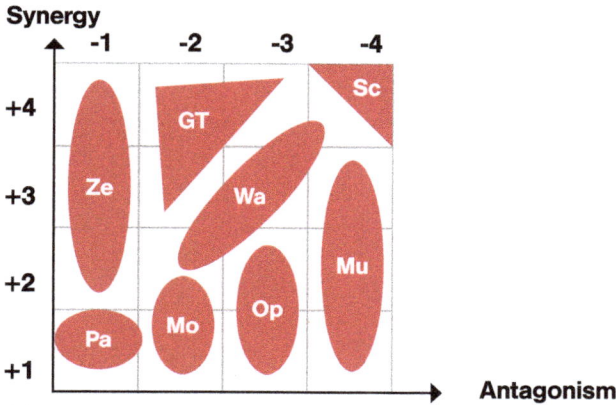

Adapted from Walley (2004)

GT = Golden Triangles *(These individuals offer helpful critical perspectives on the organisation's plans. Management can often only see negative behaviour and not the synergy. Their slight antagonism is healthy and they are strong supporters of the organisation but will continually challenge leadership.)*

Communicating with Golden Triangles: They must be given information regularly and allowed the opportunity to give feedback to management. This stakeholder grouping is critical to success. They are respected by others in the organisation as they are not seen as Zealots. If involved in communications, these individuals can adopt powerful brokering and persuasion roles by changing thinking and behaviour of the 'Waverers' and the 'Passives'.

Wa = Waverers *(These individuals are often viewed as ambivalent and apathetic to the corporate mission. But Waverers are more vocal and active than Passives. Their views (and doubts) reflect that of the passive majority. Management has a tendency to treat these individuals as two-faced and unreliable.)*

Communicating with Waverers: Waverers must be given opportunities to be listened to as they will tell the organisation exactly how they can become more supportive. Their input into communications ensures 'balanced' content. They will not act as visible ambassadors for the company mission but, if communicated with and listened to, their personal behaviour will influence the Passives.

Pa = Passives *(These individuals are disliked by Zealots and tend to be discouraging and resistant to change. Passives like order and they respect rules. They dislike uncertainty and must be allowed to ratify change. Their importance is easy to underestimate.)*

Communicating with Passives: Communication should be comprehensive and frequent. But communicators should not expect feedback, participation or even listening among these individuals. Passives cannot be forced to change behaviour. The only real way to reach them is through their neighbours. If communication is consistent, ongoing and honest, then this will lay a solid foundation for behavioural change if other stakeholder groupings are positively engaged. Passives are a paradox: they won't listen but they feel that they should be consulted about changes.

Mo = Moaners *(These individuals are sarcastic and negative towards the organisation. They moan constantly about the company and there is no easy way to please them.)*

Communicating with Moaners: Moaners may be negative but they do attend all meetings and communicators can use them as an early warning system. Participation in stakeholder groups and feedback forums is useful in identifying obstacles to the engagement of the wider workforce.

Op = Opponents *(Opponents can often be mistaken for the real ringleaders of resistance in an organisation. However, they are usually not that powerful. Unfortunately, they are individuals who will never be convinced of the organisation's true intents and will not be prepared to commit much to the collective effort.)*

Communicating with Opponents: Communication is uniform and open towards this grouping but opportunities to give feedback or participate in change activities should be kept to a minimum. Opponents are receptive to displays of strong and honest leadership – regular communication can destabilise grapevine fiction and replace it with fact but this is only for a limited time until management's focus has shifted elsewhere. Ultimately, these individuals will leave or be managed out of a successful organisation over time.

Sc = Schismatics *(Schismatics are a rare breed. Their position on any issue is extremely difficult to call, making them a highly unpredictable stakeholder group.)*

Communicating with Schismatics: Communication is consistent and accurate. The ambiguity of their views and activity makes them a phenomenal nuisance to the communication effort. Commitment is at times high and then at other times it is extremely low.

Mu = Mutineers *(Mutineers are also a tiny minority in any organisation. They are 'erratic' in nature and highly disruptive to the organisation's ambitions.)*

Communicating with Mutineers: Communication follows the same course to that of Opponents. Communication is ongoing but engagement is kept to a minimum. Ultimately, these individuals are unhappy in their roles and with the wider organisation. They will leave or be managed out of that organisation over time.

Figure 19: Socio-dynamics: Ideal influences and movement

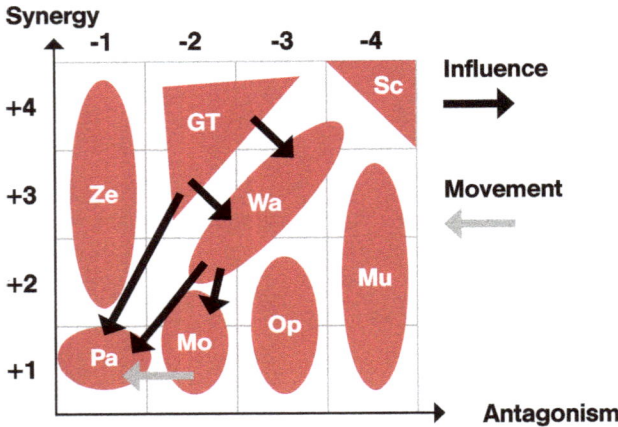

If adapted regularly and undertaken with precision, communication strategies can begin to influence and, over time, move specific stakeholder groups. Effectively, internal communicators are putting in place a system of measurement that enables segmentation and targeting for core stakeholder groups. These are key principles of marketing. Internal communicators are repackaging their product – namely the communication of key challenges and positive engagement to meet those challenges – to appeal to as many core 'internal customers' as possible.

Figure 20: Internal communication as a marketing strategy

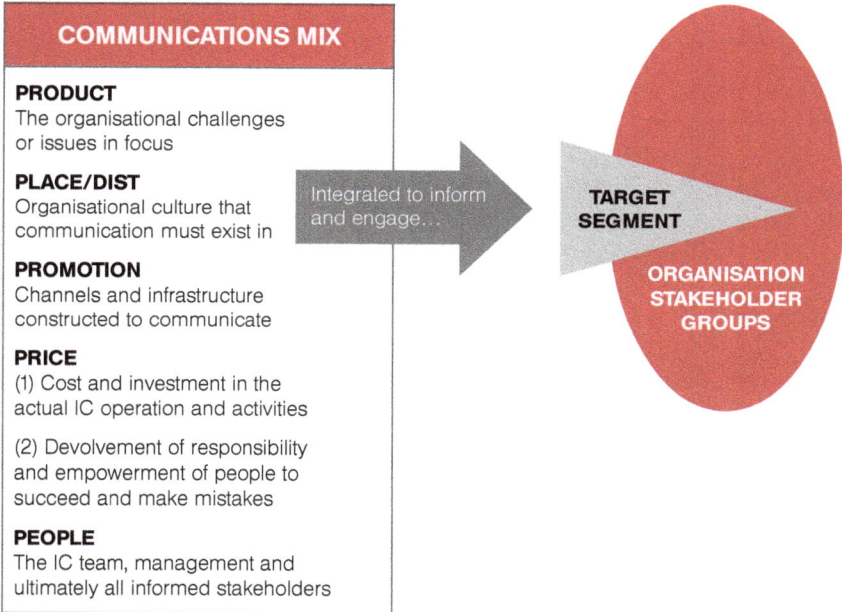

COMMUNICATIONS MIX

PRODUCT
The organisational challenges
or issues in focus

PLACE/DIST
Organisational culture that
communication must exist in

PROMOTION
Channels and infrastructure
constructed to communicate

PRICE
(1) Cost and investment in the
actual IC operation and activities

(2) Devolvement of responsibility
and empowerment of people to
succeed and make mistakes

PEOPLE
The IC team, management and
ultimately all informed stakeholders

Integrated to inform
and engage...

**TARGET
SEGMENT**

**ORGANISATION
STAKEHOLDER
GROUPS**

What value?

Visible benefits: Stakeholder analysis demonstrates a two-way approach to communication. It demonstrates a listening organisation and positively motivates employees by showing them their views and input are important. Stakeholder analysis encourages greater reciprocity since listening is an implied contract: 'I listen to you, you'll be more likely to listen to me'. An atmosphere of trust is created that moves away from command and control management.

Hidden benefits: The identification of key issues or roadblocks that are preventing employee engagement places the internal communication function at the very heart of the corporate mission.

Operations value quadrant

Service quality

Why: Every business operation must be able to track its own internal performance. Internal communication is no exception. The quality and operational effectiveness of the service it provides to the organisation must be measured for this service operation to be further improved.

Where to look:

- Internal service survey of employees
- Focus groups, employee forums and online polls
- Annual employee attitude/engagement survey
- Internal compliment/complaint analysis
- Feedback from managers and staff as to helpfulness of a specific communication to their knowledge

How to show:

- Application of Johnston & Clark's Service Quality Factor theory
- Individual quotes and references relating to service quality
- Benchmarking with similar size organisations
- Longitudinal comparisons

Service quality factors

Using Johnston & Clark's Service Quality Factor theory, communicators ask employees (or segments of their internal audience) to rate the internal communication function's performance in terms of a number of generic quality factors. Nine generic service factors are used in the example opposite.

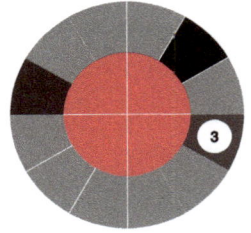

Example: Service Quality Factor (SQF) results

Stakeholder analysis

How do you rate your internal communications performance in terms of the following factors:

Figure 21: Service quality factors

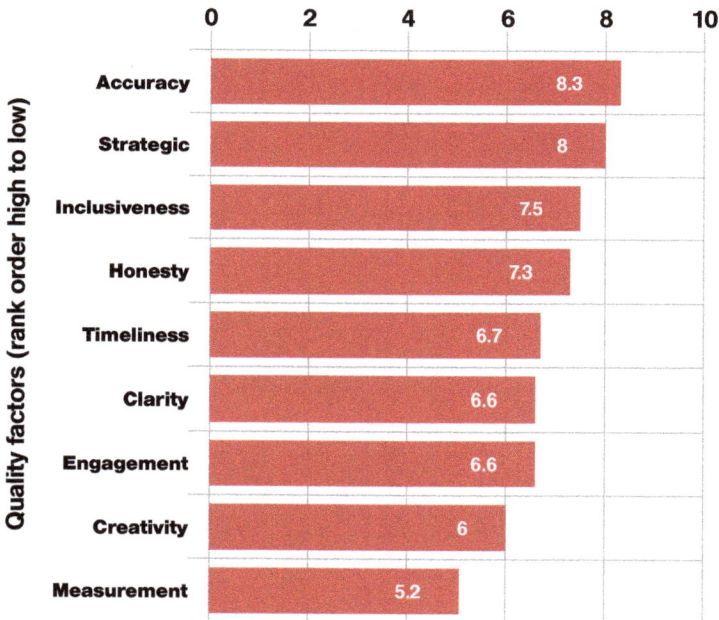

By applying Zeithaml's Zone of Tolerance theory (1993) to the factor scores, it was possible to ascertain perceived areas of strength and weakness within the internal communication service operation (see Figure 22). For the research project, Accuracy (average score: 8.3) and Strategic Alignment (average score: 8) of internal communication were both factors respondents felt were operating acceptably in their organisations. Measurement (average score: 5.2) was the poorest rated factor.

Figure 22: The zone of tolerance

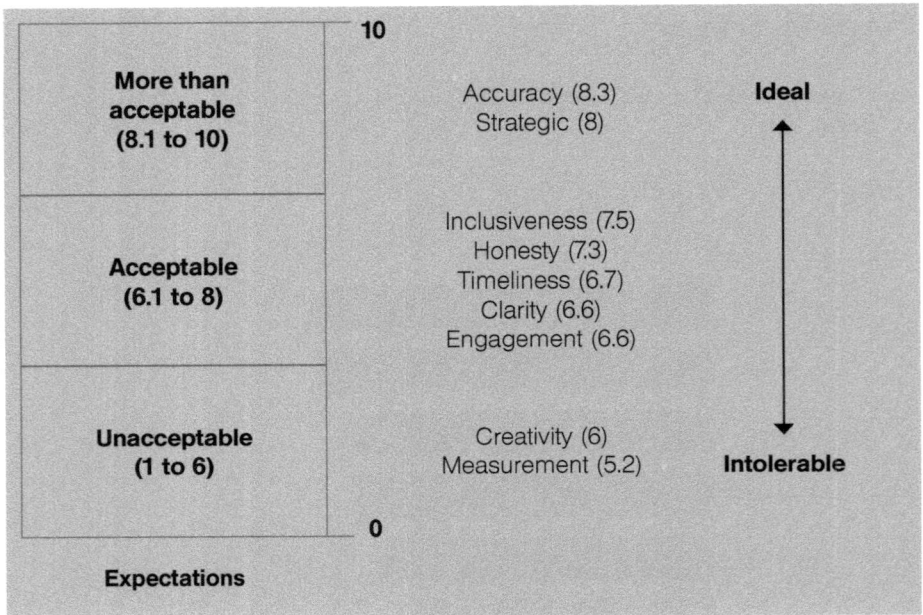

Using these results communicators can identify key service issues by classifying factors into hygiene, enhancer and critical groupings. These factors can be mapped in the following way:

Figure 23: Internal communication service quality factors

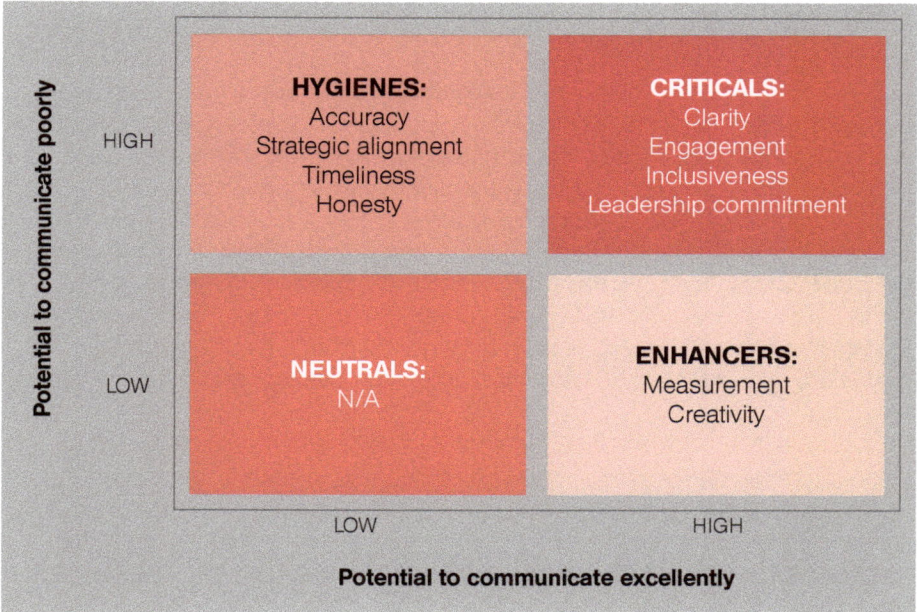

HYGIENES:
Accuracy
Strategic alignment
Timeliness
Honesty

CRITICALS:
Clarity
Engagement
Inclusiveness
Leadership commitment

NEUTRALS:
N/A

ENHANCERS:
Measurement
Creativity

Potential to communicate poorly — HIGH / LOW

Potential to communicate excellently — LOW / HIGH

Adapted from Johnston & Clark (2001)

Hygiene Factors: Accuracy, Strategic Alignment, Timeliness and Honesty are all factors that were rated as "par for the course" by respondents. Factually correct information (Accuracy) or messages that reflect senior management's future plans (Strategic Alignment) would devalue (even ruin) communication efforts rapidly if absent from the service operation.

Neutral Factors: Within the process of producing good internal communication it is arguable that no factors are neutral. All factors have impact with high potential to generate excellent or poor communication if applied or neglected within the process.

Enhancing Factors: In this example, enhancing service quality factors of Measurement and Creativity could both be used to build advantage in the communications process. In contrast to Critical or Hygiene categories, these Enhancing factors would not negatively impact communications if they were absent from day-to-day outputs. However if they are present, they do have the capacity to improve and enhance service quality. If messages are creative and entertaining they engage the recipient and hold their attention for longer. Similarly, if communication activity is measured then future efforts can be modified and improved through a continuous learning process.

Critical Factors: Lastly, Leadership Commitment, Clarity, Engagement and Inclusiveness are identified as critical communication factors that have the ability to generate effective communication or (if absent from the communication operation) to severely disrupt communication effectiveness and therefore quality.

This approach is a flexible one. The choice of service quality factors must be tailored to the requirements of the organisation and ultimately, its strategic focus. For example, if an organisation has committed to transition all its operations to a new integrated online platform or content management system (CMS) then additional service quality factors may measure aspects such as 'Navigation' of information; or 'Volume' of information etc.

What value:

Visible benefits: Tracking service quality as part of a balanced measurement model enables communicators to demonstrate value from both cost and quality perspectives. Adopting a regular, systematic approach to continual improvement of a seemingly intangible service like internal communication illustrates operational professionalism.

Hidden benefits: This practice of measuring and monitoring service quality will reveal what aspects of the internal communication service operation are really important to management. Satisfy these needs or re-educate internal customers, and communicators are building a stronger foundation for their operation.

Operational measures

The five main performance objectives of any operation are Quality, Speed, Dependability, Flexibility and Cost (Slack & Chambers, 2001). These objectives are made up of a collection of smaller related measures, so they are broken down into constituent parts. For example:

Speed

1 Actual versus theoretical production cycle of newsletter
2 Frequency of communication channels events/output
3 Time taken to deliver messages and collect feedback
4 Daily time required to update news section of intranet
5 Response time to internal enquiries/requests

This process of disaggregating the overall objectives leads to measurable performance indicators. Measurement can be further qualified by identifying two basic types of measure:

* Variables (measured on a continuously variable scale)
* Attributes (assessed by judgement and dichotomous e.g. Yes/No)

A set of core operational measures can be developed for the internal communication function and its main communications operational process. For example:

Once defined and updated regularly, the measures reflect the relevant standards set for the specific operation undertaken. Each should be aligned to the main priorities of the internal communication strategy as a whole. Measuring operational and service quality performance will reveal areas of performance that are below expectations and in need of improvement.

Figure 24: Performance area example – intranet

OPERATIONAL VARIABLE	ATTRIBUTE	OBJECTIVE
QUALITY	The organisational challenges or issues in focus	Do users find the website/ intranet/app of regular use/value? (Y/N)
SPEED	Daily time required to update news section of the intranet? (Mins/hours)	Is the news posted within 24 hours of an event happening? (Y/N)
DEPENDABILITY	How many times and for how long has the intranet been down in past quarter? (Numerical figure/time)	Do users have consistently easy access to the intranet? (Y/N)
FLEXIBILITY	Response time to internal submissions for the intranet? (Numerical figure)	Does the intranet adequately reflect local views across the business? (Y/N)
COST	Cost of maintaining the intranet (content team and technical/support)? (£)	Is the cost associated with the intranet within projected budget?

Other ways to measure value

There now follow nine more examples of how internal communications value can be demonstrated. These examples fit within the four quadrants and complete a balanced value framework. They are not exhaustive. They are intended to be a flexible set of measures. It is up to each internal communicator to decide which mix of measures works best for their organisation.

Figure 25:

External value quadrant

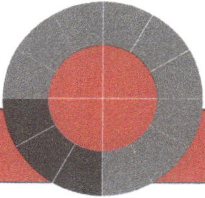

CUSTOMER	
WHY?	Customer focus is a company-wide activity. Internal communication must be able to link its activities to the customer and the quantifiable benefits this activity generates.
WHERE TO LOOK?	• Customer satisfaction surveys and reports • Marketing research/analysis (focus groups/surveys) • Compliment/complaint analysis • Press coverage of employee events and activities
HOW TO SHOW?	• Link customer satisfaction with profitability and employee engagement levels – a series of quarterly scores • Show where key operational issues are being communicated internally (then further link with changes in behaviour and performance)
WHAT VALUE?	**Visible benefits:** Internal communication is showing practical applications that have positive impacts on customer service performance. **Hidden benefits:** Internal communication is supporting increased employee branding which in some organisations is a sustainable competitive advantage.

Figure 26:

External value quadrant

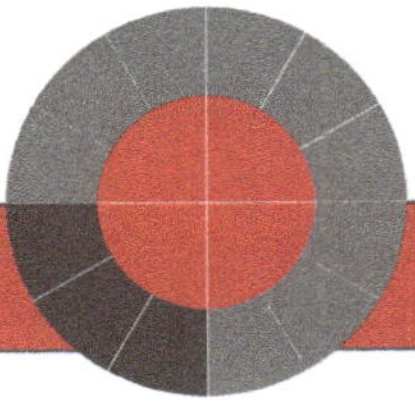

PARTNERS AND SUPPLIERS	
WHY?	In today's economy effective alliances and partnering relationships are driving success, as organisations realise they cannot be specialists in every department of the value chain. Outsourcing IT and non-core services creates large numbers of 'indirect employees'. The need to communicate effectively with this wider 'team' is critical to generating efficient and committed cross-business relationships at all levels.
WHERE TO LOOK?	• Supplier relationship agreements • Contractual performance levels • Project reports • Alliance teams – communication activity provided • Individual feedback
HOW TO SHOW?	• Comparisons of alliance performance • Relationship mapping exercises • Number of project/work stoppages • Showcase new starter communications activity • Personal quotes from partners/suppliers • Financial analysis: cost/benefit analysis
WHAT VALUE?	**Visible benefits:** Internal communication is playing an important part in generating positive partnering relationships. **Hidden benefits:** This is an increasingly relevant and important side to internal communication activity. Outsourced service employees and general suppliers are also indirect ambassadors for the organisation. There are multiple benefits to informing and involving them through good internal communication practice.

Figure 27:

External value quadrant

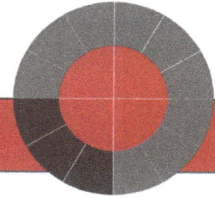

	FUTURE ADVANTAGE		
WHY?	Looking outside of the immediate organisation presents an opportunity to show what the latest trends are in the field of internal communication and how other organisations may be benefitting already. Like any other part of an organisation the function must strive to be innovative in its activities. Critically, care must be taken to relate these trends and examples of best practice back to the organisation. The internal communication operation should ultimately aim to make itself a critical area of sustainable competitive advantage.		
WHERE TO LOOK?	• Group/industry associations and alliances • Award competitions • Marketing analysis: Competitor analyses • Trade publications • Specialist communications forums and networking events • Communications consultants • Site visits to other companies of similar size		
HOW TO SHOW?	• Individual case studies (featuring parallels to the organisation's own situation) • Industry/geographic trend in investment levels • Judges' critiques • Benchmarking studies		
WHAT VALUE?	**Visible benefits:** Demonstration of forward-thinking, innovative approach to improving the operation. **Hidden benefits:** Demonstrating that internal communication can be a sustainable competitive advantage.		

Figure 28:

Employee value quadrant

EMPLOYEE ENGAGEMENT	
WHY?	Employee attitude and satisfaction is the common foundation for demonstrating internal communication effectiveness. But what's really important is tracking levels of knowledge and actual behaviour (Likely, 2004). A well-informed workforce is an involved and loyal workforce. Employee engagement measures (performed regularly) will reveal changes in behaviour. It will help identify 'what' and 'why' people are thinking in a specific way and lend weight to increased emphasis n communication activities.
WHERE TO LOOK?	• Annual staff engagement survey • PDP and appraisal feedback • Employee turnover and attrition levels • Absenteeism and sickness • Intranet hit rates • Readership pulse surveys
HOW TO SHOW?	• Numerical scores of commitment levels • Ratio analysis • Comparisons with previous quarter/year • Links to employee turnover and organisational performance • Individual quotes and case examples
WHAT VALUE?	**Visible benefits:** Enhancement of traditional staff satisfaction surveys that will ultimately reveal general levels of commitment. In many organisations this will form part of a Balanced Business Scorecard performance management system. **Hidden benefits:** Engagement is more relevant to the strategic business agenda. Satisfaction (though important) is not a direct measure of internal communication value. Engagement measures update this traditional internal communication measure and put it in context – as one part of a more practical, balanced system of value indicators.

Figure 29:

Employee value quadrant

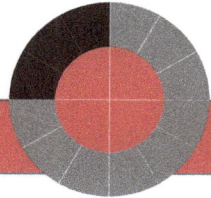

	IDEAS AND INNOVATION	
WHY?	When IBM took over Lotus in the mid-1990s, the eventual purchase price was US$3.5 billion – far above the actual market value of Lotus itself (US$250 million). The reason behind this seemingly inflated valuation was the demonstrable value of Lotus's staff and their intellectual capital. Employee innovation and creativity is an essential aspect of any organisation in today's knowledge economy. Internal communication must be involved in facilitating the flow of ideas across all organisational lines – in terms of both volume and speed.	
WHERE TO LOOK?	• Suggestion schemes • Comment boxes • Online polls and campaign responses • Employee surveys • Internal competitions • Open forums • Working groups • Communities of Practice	
HOW TO SHOW?	• Numerical volumes of ideas • Comparisons with previous quarter/year • Cost/benefit analysis • Links to productivity and organisational performance • Individual quotes and case examples	
WHAT VALUE?	**Visible benefits:** Promotion of ideas and innovation leads to business improvement and increased staff morale. Aligning internal communication activity to operational improvements demonstrates the essential role the function has to play in the development and growth of the organisation. **Hidden benefits:** Encouraging the healthy flow of ideas and suggestions is part of a wider two-way communication culture and underlines a need for internal communication activity.	

Figure 30:

Leadership value quadrant

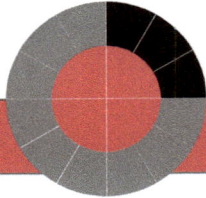

ADVICE AND TRAINING	
WHY?	Through general analysis of management performance, internal communicators can identify areas where improvement is needed with regard to individual skills training. Liaison with HR to address gaps in individual communications skills followed by the arrangement of communications workshops, lunchtime briefings or an online or telephone advice service positions internal communicators as specialists in their organisation.
WHERE TO LOOK?	• PDP and appraisal systems • 360 reviews • Employee survey and communication/culture audits • HR reports and observations • Employee exit interviews • Management feedback, forums and conferences
HOW TO SHOW?	• Number/description of workshops arranged • Testimonials from attendees as to benefits • Longitudinal comparisons of appraisals, 360s and employee surveys
WHAT VALUE?	**Visible benefits:** Improvement of managers' basic communications skills will aid the daily operational effort. **Hidden benefits:** Greater appreciation and advocacy of internal communication within the management line. Implicit positioning of internal communication as the functional specialist.

Figure 31:

Leadership value quadrant

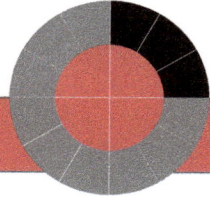

	FINANCIAL MANAGEMENT
WHY?	Senior leadership responds best to hard facts in any business situation. Internal communication professionals must be able to demonstrate value for money through effective financial management. Operating within a set budget – even generating a small percentage saving – should be shown to senior levels of the organisation.
WHERE TO LOOK?	• Department budget performance – actual vs forecast • Discussions with suppliers – % discount savings through contractual agreements with preferred suppliers • Market and industry intelligence
HOW TO SHOW?	• Ratio analysis: Turnover: Communications budget (tracked against cost of inflation) • Ratio analysis: Profit per employee linked to spend on internal communication per employee • Unit cost of communication items – year on year comparisons • Email: Cost vs time equation • Comparisons internally with other functional spends • Benchmarking with similar size organisations
WHAT VALUE?	**Visible benefits:** Demonstration of value for money and effective cost management. Enhances internal perceptions of the function as a professional, results-oriented discipline. **Hidden benefits:** Harder fiscal comparisons strike a chord with senior leadership. Any argument of increased investment in internal communication must be built upon sound financial data. Assuming a zero-budgeting perspective instills fiscal accountability and negates fears of wasting resource.

Figure 32:

Operations value quadrant

PROJECT SUPPORT	
WHY?	Professional communicators fail to demonstrate just how much value they add to the organisation through consistent involvement with various project teams. Internal communication functions must make the link with practical business outcomes. Demonstrating project involvement encourages equal status with operational management levels and changes general perceptions of the function. This input and effort must not go unseen as it is highly valuable.
WHERE TO LOOK?	• Operational performance results • Personal timesheets • Project meeting minutes and actions • Specific communications output for projects • Testimonial from project leaders as to benefits
HOW TO SHOW?	• Quantifiable breakdown of time spent in project work • Display of key results from operational projects • Display of communication material delivered to support projects • Quotes relating to value of comms from project leaders
WHAT VALUE?	**Visible benefits:** By recurrently linking activity to practical project output (e.g. a safety project that has helped to reduce accident levels), internal communication is demonstrating more tangible business value. **Hidden benefits:** Positioning of the function at an advisory level with adequate opportunity to influence decision-making. This in turn improves internal communicator's overall understanding of the real operational business issues.

Figure 33:

Operations value quadrant

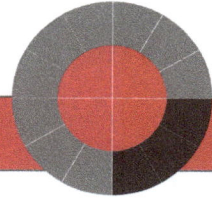

	PERFORMANCE INDICATORS
WHY?	You can't manage what you don't measure. Every business operation must be able to track its own internal performance. Internal communication is no exception. The operational effectiveness of its processes must be measured in order to be further improved. This is critical to ensure that the operation reflects how the organisation is developing.
WHERE TO LOOK?	• Internal service survey of employees or key stakeholders • IT performance data – hit rates, down time etc. • Team timesheet information • Readership surveys/reports/focus groups • Line reporting mechanisms – individual PDPs
HOW TO SHOW?	• Operational objectives measurement • Target performance standards • Longitudinal comparisons (quarterly/annually) • Benchmarking with similar size organisations
WHAT VALUE?	**Visible benefits:** Tracking actual operational performance as part of a balanced measurement model enables communicators to demonstrate value from both cost and quality perspectives. Adopting a regular, systematic approach to continual improvement of specific internal communication operations demonstrates visible professionalism as well as maximum value for money. **Hidden benefits:** This practice guards against damaging internal perceptions surrounding what internal communication actually does. It enhances the case for investment.

STEP 4: **Present the value**

The next step is to present the value of internal communication activity in as efficient and attention-grabbing manner as possible to senior leaders, then wider management levels.

Outlined in the preceding section were a number of suggested indicators of value. The four value quadrants of the model provide a simple and concise structure to any report or presentation undertaken by the internal communication function to show its value.

These should be presented visually through selective text and graphical description. No one value quadrant is over-represented. The way in which measurement data is displayed is a key means of helping to achieve its purpose but this should not eclipse the main value outcomes that the report or presentation seeks to demonstrate.

Stake a claim: Part of the real problem for internal communicators is arguably self-made. They are unwilling to claim links with outward business performance because they feel that the influence of internal communication is too indirect to be credible. But isn't corporate success a team effort?

The value of communications may be indirect but it is present and contributory nonetheless. Internal communicators must not be afraid to show how their function has contributed to the collective success of a particular project or a specific performance outcome.

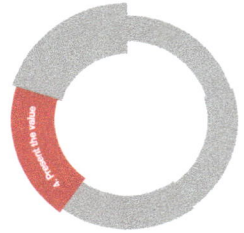

Figure 34: Internal communication service quality factors

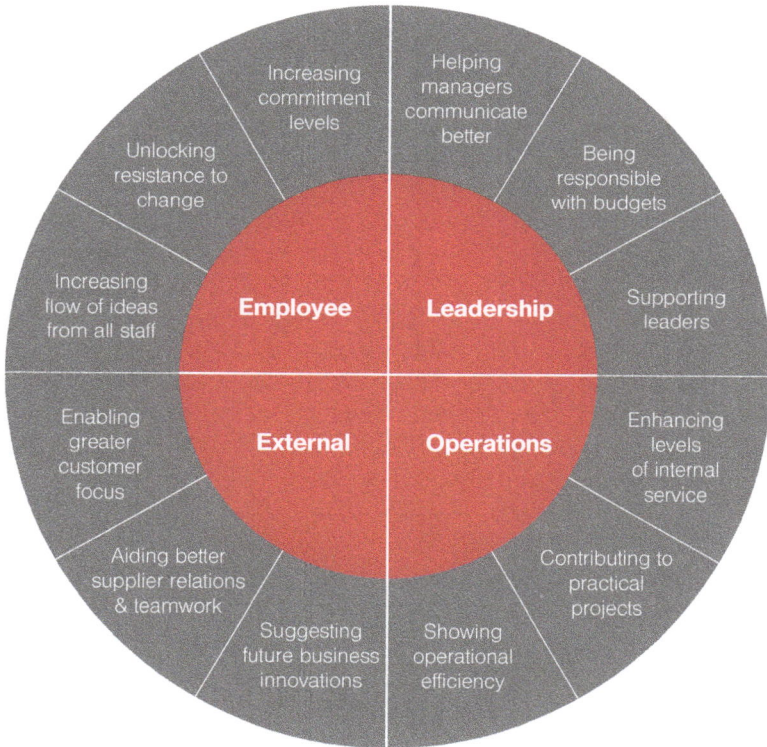

Ashby (2005)

Many operational functions are taken for granted in organisations because they are deemed 'non-core'. This classification is a matter of perception. Facilities management or IT support may not directly contribute to the bottom line but they would soon bring a business to a grinding halt if absent from day-to-day operations. Like every other operational function, internal communication must demonstrate its worth to the rest of an organisation in a balanced and professional manner. Crucially, it must strive to move from being a necessary operational function to one that is seen as pivotal to success. Demonstrating a measured array of value-adding activities and visible outcomes in the context of a wider team is a necessary step to achieving this objective.

Quarterly reporting: Presenting the value must be a regular and standard procedure. A quarterly frequency of reporting is recommended. Internal communicators should produce a concise performance report for the senior executive of their organisation. This should be presented to the Board as part of the organisation's strategic performance and incorporated in middle and senior management briefings as a standard quarterly practice.

It may be a truism but any balanced approach to performance measurement needs to be used and updated regularly to be fully effective. Balanced scorecards fail when, having developed strategic goals and identified relevant performance measures, an enterprise does not use the information provided to drive changes in the way the organisation works (Schneiderman, 1999). The same is true for this value framework. If communicators do not persistently demonstrate the value of their activities and actively improve the way they work they will not have a sustainable foundation with which to take their discipline forward.

STEP 5: Create the circle

If this is undertaken comprehensively, a virtuous circle for internal communication value is created. Regular reporting will generate a balanced set of value indicators and outcomes that are aligned to the business strategy.

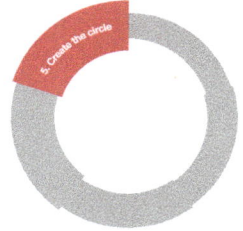

Figure 35: Virtuous circle for Internal Communication value

1: ORGANISATIONAL LEVEL

Benefits:

- Clarity of purpose across the entire workforce

2: OPERATIONAL LEVEL

Benefits:

- Strategic alignment
- Operational efficiency
- Focus of effort

3: VALUE LEVEL

Benefits:

- Internal credibility
- Review & improvement

Ashby (2005)

STEP 5: **Create the circle**

Once in place, this framework will be efficient to maintain and flexible enough to accommodate desired changes in organisational objectives and structure. The value framework takes account of the organisation's strategic objectives which in turn naturally encourage clarity of purpose across the entire workforce. As well as being strategically aligned, all internal communication operations are more accountable. Limited time and resources are channelled in the right places to maximise effort.

Regularly demonstrating value-based activities builds internal credibility and perceived importance. Internal communication begins to take a central position at the heart of the organisation. The framework provides a platform for internal communication professionals to review and enhance their performance against the changing needs of the organisation. This process of continual improvement completes the virtuous circle (see Figure 35).

The Five Step Value Framework presented in this book has genuine and valuable applications in the field of internal communication. All too often professional communicators overlook the best ways to communicate what they do and then wonder why greater support from management is not forthcoming.

If the discipline of internal communication is to develop further then its exponents need to establish a flexible model from which to measure and demonstrate their worth to the rest of the organisation. The Five Step Value Framework offers a practical and balanced approach to achieving this.

The Five Step Value Framework

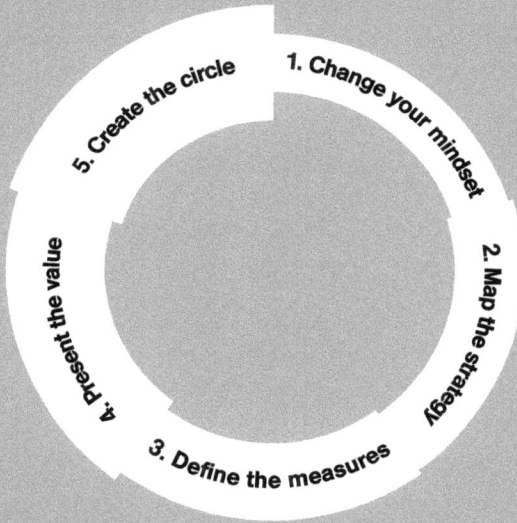

A circular diagram showing:
- 1. Change your mindset
- 2. Map the strategy
- 3. Define the measures
- 4. Present the value
- 5. Create the circle

Selected bibliography

Atkinson, J. (1967) 'A handbook for interviewers: a manual for Government Social Survey interviewing staff, describing practice and procedures on structured interviewing' (Government Social Survey, no. M136.), H.M.S.O, London.

Brignall, S. et al (1999) 'Improving Service Performance: A Study of Step-Change Versus Continuous Improvement', CIMA, London, 1999.

Cannell & Kahn as referenced in Lindzey, G. & Aronson, E. (1968) 'The Handbook of Social Psychology', Vol. 5 Applied Social Psychology.

Dibb, S. et al (2001) 'Marketing Concepts and Strategies', Houghton Mifflin, Boston.

Downs, C. (1988) 'Communication Audits', Glenview, Ill.: Scott Foresman. 1. Moser, C.A. & Kalton, G. (1986) 'Survey Methods in Social Investigation', Gower Publishing, Aldershot, UK.

Faulkner, D. (2002) Taken from Strategic Advantage Module course slides (Week 4).

Fowler, F.J. & Mangione, T.W. (1990) 'Standardized Survey Interviewing: Minimizing Interviewer-related Type Error', Applied Social Research Methods Series Vol. 18. Sage, Newbury Park, California.

Gatley, L. & Clutterbuck, D. (1996) 'The Strategic Management of Internal Communication', Business Intelligence, London.

Hargie, O. & Tourish, D. (2000) 'Handbook of Communication Audits for Organisations', Routledge, London.

Hayes, R. H. & Wheelwright, S.C. (1984) 'Restoring Our Competitive Edge', John Wiley Press.

Hill, T. (1993) 'Manufacturing Strategy', Macmillan, London.

Johnston, R. & Clark, G. (2001) 'Service Operations Management', Prentice Hall.

Kaplan, R. S. & Norton, D. P. 'The Balanced Scorecard – Measures That Drive Performance', Harvard Business Review, Jan-Feb, 1992, pp. 71-9.

King, N. (1994) 'The qualitative research interview', in Cassell, C. & Symon, G. (eds) 'Qualitative Methods in Organisational Research: A Practical Guide', Sage, London.

Likely, F. (2004) 'Ten things we should know about evaluation', Strategic Communications Management, Volume 8, Issue 5, Aug/Sept 2004, Melcrum Publishing, London.

Schneiderman, A. M. (1999) 'Why balanced scorecards fail', Journal of Strategic Performance Measurement, January Special Edition: 6.

Shaw, K. (2004) 'Revealing the fault lines in communication measurement', Strategic Communications Management, Volume 8, Issue 5, Aug/Sept 2004, Melcrum Publishing, London.

Slack, N. Chambers, S. & Johnston, R. (2001) 'Operations Management', Prentice Hall (Harlow).

Staughton, R. (2004) 'The Relationship Continuum'.

Stewart, D. & Shamdasani, P. N. (1990) 'Focus groups: theory and practice', Sage, London.

Tufte, E. R. (1983) 'The Visual Display of Quantitative Information', Graphics Press, Connecticut.

Walley, P. (2004) 'Stakeholder behaviour – measuring social-dynamics using Fauvet's theory', Taken from Project Management Module course slides (Day 4).

Zeithaml, V. A. et al (1993) 'The Nature and Determinants of Customer Expectations of Service', Journal of the Academy of Marketing Science, Vol. 21, No. 1.

About the author

Corin Ashby MBA, FIIC has been helping businesses improve their internal communication since 1996. During that time he has worked with many leading communications practitioners from private and public sectors in both the UK and USA.

Corin was associate partner at employee engagement specialist Trident Communications before setting up 44 Communications. He holds a first-class MBA from Warwick Business School and is a fellow of the Institute of Internal Communication (IoIC).

The Five Step Value Framework

is now also available as an interactive online resource.

To access this online white paper, please visit: www.fsvf.co.uk

Other business titles published by Mosaïque Press –

Essential reading from the Marketing Mentor

Alastair Campbell, the Marketing Mentor, has established a reputation for clear, insightful business advice through his speaking, writing, radio and TV work and mentoring. He shares his insights in three books that offer practical ways to build your business.

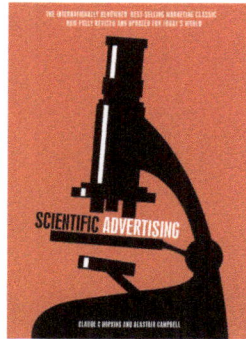

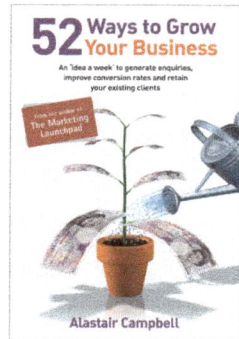

The Marketing Launchpad
The six most powerful marketing areas that you need to understand to launch your business into a new orbit.

52 Ways to Grow Your Business
'An idea a week' for generating enquiries, improving conversion rates and retaining your exiting clients.

Scientific Advertising
Claude C Hopkins' classic on the art of advertising, revised and updated for today's marketplace by Alastair Campbell.

Available from Amazon and other online retailers.

MOSAÏQUEPRESS

www.ingramcontent.com/pod-product-compliance
Lightning Source LLC
Chambersburg PA
CBHW042350040426
42449CB00018B/3474